EMOTIONS

Sad

by Kirsten Chang

BLASTOFF! READERS 1

BELLWETHER MEDIA • MINNEAPOLIS, MN

Blastoff! Readers are carefully developed by literacy experts to build reading stamina and move students toward fluency by combining standards-based content with developmentally appropriate text.

Level 1 provides the most support through repetition of high-frequency words, light text, predictable sentence patterns, and strong visual support.

Level 2 offers early readers a bit more challenge through varied sentences, increased text load, and text-supportive special features.

Level 3 advances early-fluent readers toward fluency through increased text load, less reliance on photos, advancing concepts, longer sentences, and more complex special features.

★ **Blastoff! Universe**

This edition first published in 2025 by Bellwether Media, Inc.

Library of Congress Cataloging-in-Publication Data

LC record for Sad available at: https://lccn.loc.gov/2024014733

Editor: Rebecca Sabelko Designer: Andrea Schneider

Printed in the United States of America, North Mankato, MN.

Table of Contents

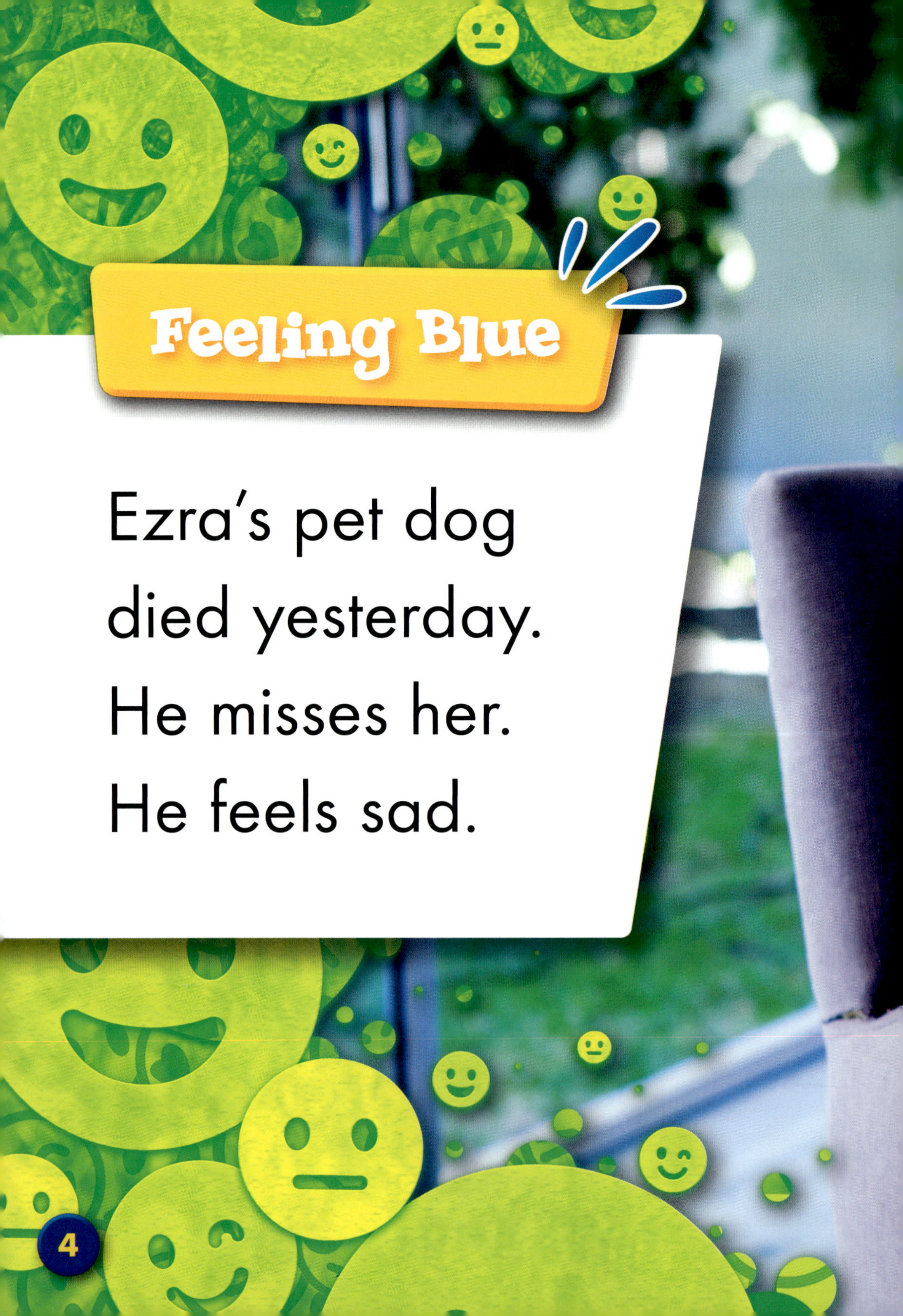

Feeling Blue

Ezra's pet dog
died yesterday.
He misses her.
He feels sad.

What Is Sadness?

Sadness is an emotion. You feel unhappy when you are sad.

Down or blue are other names for sadness.

Brian loses a game. He feels **disappointed**.

Lily's friend moves away.
Lily plays alone more.
This makes her sad.

Why Are You Sad?

a loved one dying

losing a game

a friend moving away

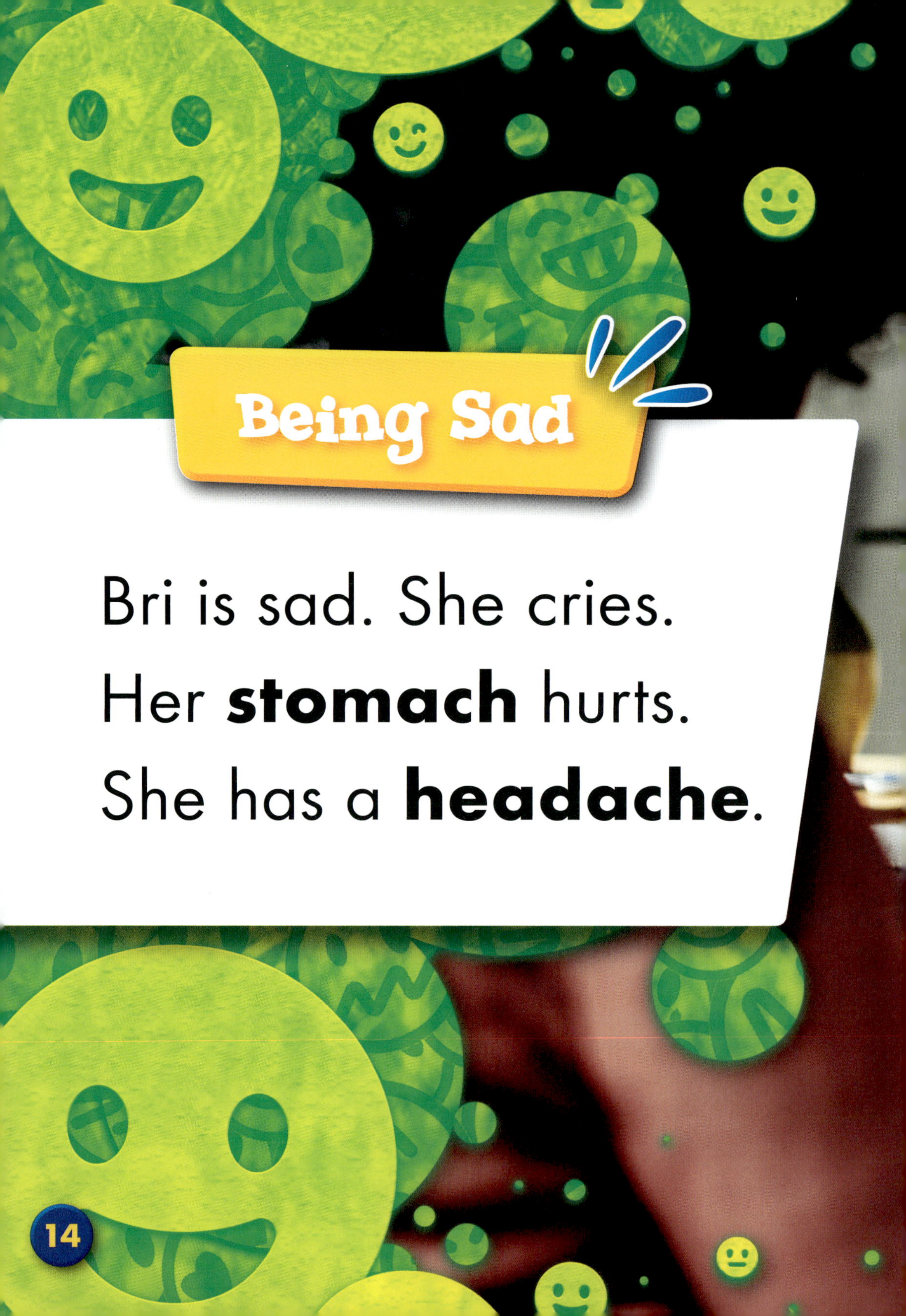

Being Sad

Bri is sad. She cries.
Her **stomach** hurts.
She has a **headache**.

Kylie feels down.
She **frowns**.
She looks
at the ground.

Identify Sadness

crying

having a stomachache

frowning

Sadness can make you feel sleepy. You feel like you have no **energy**.

It is okay to feel sad.
It helps to talk
to someone you trust.

What makes you feel sad?

Glossary

disappointed

unhappy because something you hoped for did not happen

headache

pain in the head

energy

strength that helps you do things

stomach

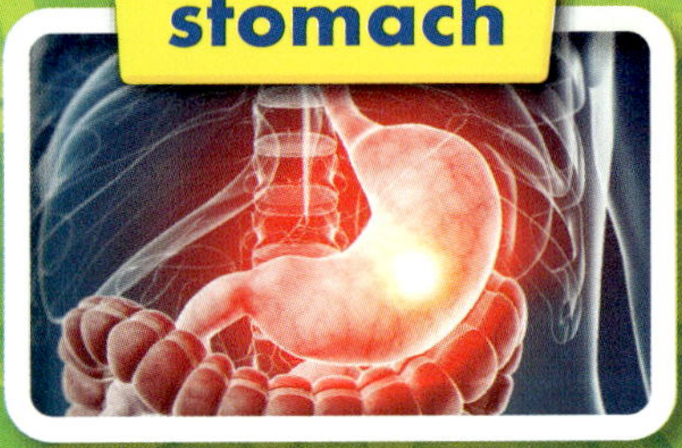

a part of the body that breaks down food

frowns

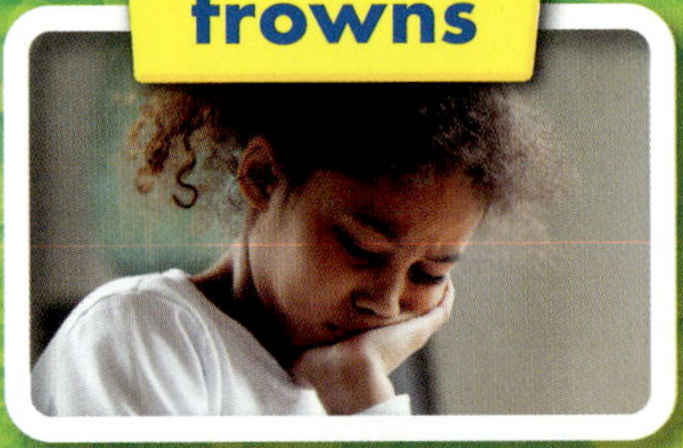

brings eyebrows together, showing a person is upset or thinking

To Learn More

AT THE LIBRARY

Chang, Kirsten. *Understanding Emotions*. Minneapolis, Minn.: Bellwether Media, 2022.

Culliford, Amy. *Sad*. New York, N.Y.: Crabtree Publishing Company, 2022.

Lake, Theia. *Feeling Sad*. Buffalo, N.Y.: Enslow Publishing, 2023.

ON THE WEB

FACTSURFER

Factsurfer.com gives you a safe, fun way to find more information.

1. Go to www.factsurfer.com.
2. Enter "sad" into the search box and click 🔍.
3. Select your book cover to see a list of related content.

Index

The images in this book are reproduced through the courtesy of: AntonioDiaz, front cover (sad child); Evgenyatamanenko, front cover (background); khosrork, p. 3; wavebreakmedia, pp. 4-5; Pixel-Shot, pp. 6-7; howtogoto, pp. 8-9; Brocreative, pp. 10-11; Ольга Чуприна, pp. 12-13; Ruslan Huzau, p. 13 (a loved one dying); Fotokostic, p. 13 (losing a game); Tomsickova Tatyana, p. 13 (a friend moving away); jeffbergen, pp. 14-15; aldomurillo, pp. 16-17; LightField Studios, p. 17 (crying); Aleksandra Suzi, p. 17 (having a stomachache); LN team, p. 17 (frowning); :staticnak1983, pp. 18-19; DimaBerlin, pp. 20-21; Nomad_Soul, p. 22 (disappointed); Sharomka, p. 22 (energy); fizkes, p. 22 (frowns); 220 Selfmade studio, p. 22 (headache); Sebastian Kaulitzki, p. 22 (stomach); SumeetK/peopleimages.com, p. 23 (sad child).